EXCLUSIVE INTERVIEWS WITH
RON POLK & SKIP BERTMAN

FROM THE CREATOR OF
MENTAL GAME VIP

MATT MORSE

Coaching Legends VIP:

Exclusive Interviews with Ron Polk & Skip Bertman

Printed in the United States of America

Published by Compete Publishing

Author/Creator: Matt Morse

ISBN-13: 978-0-9969367-2-9

ABOUT THE CREATOR

Matt Morse is an entrepreneur, coach, consultant, author, and speaker. He is a former NCAA Division 1 student-athlete who always had aspirations of coaching at the collegiate level following his playing career. During Matt's 5 years on the baseball team at UAB, Ron Polk served as the Blazers' volunteer assistant coach.

After creating Mental Game VIP, an extensive research project that goes deep inside the minds of baseball's best mental performance coaches, Matt decided to utilize the same interview format with a focus on coaching at the collegiate level with two of the game's legendary coaches.

Matt's passion for the game of baseball and helping others become the best they can be on and off the field is strongly evident throughout his coaching and training of highly competitive athletes.

In addition to coaching, Matt also consults with and speaks to teams, organizations, coaches, and athletes around the world. For more information on Matt, to have him come speak to you and your team, or if you want to create your own VIP collection, visit **Matt-Morse.com** and follow @MattMorse_17 on Twitter!

Pictured Above: Matt (left) and his wife Rachel (right) with Coach Polk (middle) at the 2015 UAB Baseball Banuqet

CONTENTS

WHAT INSPIRED YOU TO BECOME A COACH?

DID YOU HAVE STANDARDS/EXPECTATIONS FOR YOUR TEAMS?

HOW DID YOU MOTIVATE YOUR TEAM AND GET THEM ALL MOVING IN THE SAME DIRECTION?

WHAT DOES THE 'IT' FACTOR LOOK LIKE? WHEN A KID HAS IT, HOW DO YOU HARNESS AND EMPOWER IT?

WHAT WAS YOUR RECRUITING PHILOSOPHY?

WHO WERE THE MENTORS OR COACHES THAT MADE THE GREATEST IMPACT ON YOUR LIFE?

HOW DID YOU BALANCE YOUR PERSONAL AND PROFESSIONAL LIFE WITH THE DEMANDS OF BEING A HEAD BASEBALL COACH?

WHAT DOES IT TAKE TO BE A GREAT BASEBALL COACH?

WHAT IS YOUR PROUDEST MOMENT? WHY?

COACHING LEGENDS VIP DEFINED

The Coaching Legends VIP Program features a pair of interviews with legendary college baseball coaches Ron Polk and Skip Bertman. These audio interviews have been transcribed and sorted by topic for you to read, or simply reference while listening to the corresponding audio.

Meet the Coaches contains a set of specific questions for each featured coach. The **Q&A** is a series of questions asked to each coach and includes their various responses to these frequently asked questions among the baseball coaching community. Both Polk and Bertman were then put on the **HotSeat**, where they were asked to provide their initial thoughts on several popular topics. **The Conclusion** contains recommended reading and closing comments from each coach.

The material covered in this program covers a wide variety of topics that are extremely beneficial to college baseball players, coaches, parents, fans and especially aspiring coaches. Get to know both Coach Polk and Coach Bertman inside Coaching Legends VIP!

*Interviews have been modified and condensed by the VIP team.

A FORMER PLAYER'S PERSPECTIVE
by Dr. Bhrett McCabe

McCabe: I wouldn't be where I'm at today if it wasn't for Skip Bertman. It is an impact that continues today. Skip gave me a chance when I was not highly recruited. I only played one year of varsity baseball, but he believed in me. He believed in his system and he believed in people who buy into his system. There is a reason why he was as successful as he was.

Everything had to be excellent from the time the opposing team got off the bus, which is funny because he didn't make us clean up our shoes. A lot of coaches spend a lot of time on how clean your shoes are. Skip didn't care about that, but he cared about how clean the field looked, how clean the batting cages looked, how tight the strings were around the cages that were out on the field. When we walked out to the field, everybody was wearing the same thing. We didn't practice in shorts because you don't play in shorts. Your bullpen sessions, as pitchers, had to be excellent. There was a plan. There was a way to go about warming up. There was a way about getting into the rhythm of the bullpen. Everything had a structure to it and I use that today.

He didn't care about the things that didn't matter, like your shoes being clean. He didn't care about that. He didn't care if your hat had sweat rings on it. He didn't care if you had facial hair. He'd tease you but he didn't care about that.

At a baseball clinic I heard him say, "Coaches spend so much time trying to understand how a player runs through first base and break it down, so that maybe one time in their career the guy can make it to second base on their overthrow. Who cares? Teach the kid how to hit the three-run home run."

He cared about the big things. If you showed up at LSU, he wanted you to be impressed by how crisp everything was, and how good the concession stands were. Everything! I walk into businesses or I'll get an email from an organization and there is a misspelling or the message isn't clear. I'm thinking 'Wow, what a terrible first impression.' He wanted everything to be done like that and he pushed us for excellence.

He took risks on players because he believed if people fell into their system they would work out. There is a football coach in the state of Alabama who is very similar to that.

DR. McCABE ON COACH POLK

Coach Polk was a legend. He was the only coach I knew who looked like his mascot and he was the only coach I knew who wore spikes during a game. He wore number one, which I always thought was funny because it tells you who is in charge of their organization. I have so much respect for Coach Polk. He is the godfather of SEC baseball.

I remember pitching in the SEC tournament in Oxford, Mississippi and after I'd gotten injured my throwing motion had gone to really terrible places but it worked. My shoulder hurt, so I had a really herky-jerky throwing motion. I remember warming up in the bullpen and Polk's team, Mississippi State, was playing after us. I got done and Ron just looked at me and goes, "God, my arms hurts just watching you throw." But, I always did well against him. His teams were full of good guys. I played with them in summer ball. It is kind of a cousin tree for the LSU baseball team. We came from the same systems of Ron Fraser at Miami.

Coach Polk is just a tremendous man with a tremendous heart. He always fought hard for the student athlete in baseball. In the NCAA, everybody ignores us like we are the ugly step children in the NCAA with only 11.7 scholarships. I think my sophomore year, he resigned from Mississippi State in protest and he was dead on the money. I wish more men would stand up like him in what he fought for with the student athletes in baseball. You have great athletes playing this game that go on to do great things and we are absolutely shafted by the NCAA. It is an organization that doesn't get it. They don't understand it. They want us to be like hockey. Northeastern schools should not compete with the SEC or teams in the Southeast. It is just different, but we shouldn't compete with their hockey programs either. There is no equitable things going on for LSU to have the same hockey program as Michigan-Upper Peninsula and they just assume it is inequitable, but in baseball they try to force it. Ron never accepted that. He believed that we should fight for the way it should be done and anyone who stands out on a limb like that for thousands of athletes he doesn't even know, I will tip my cap to that man any day.

Dr. Bhrett McCabe played for Skip Bertman at LSU from 1991-1995. He won two College World Series national championships and was a member of three SEC championship teams. It was a result of his playing career and his own struggles overcoming injuries that led him to pursue a career in injury rehabilitation, performance, and sport psychology. Learn more about Dr. Bhrett McCabe at www.BhrettMcCabe.com.

MEET THE COACHES

COACHES

Introductions + Exclusive Q&A

RON POLK

LEGENDARY COLLEGE BASEBALL COACH AND THE 'FATHER OF SEC BASEBALL'

- WINNINGEST COACH IN MISSISSIPPI STATE AND SEC HISTORY IN ALL SPORTS
- REACHED THE COLLEGE WORLD SERIES 8 TIMES IN 5 DIFFERENT DECADES
- 187 FORMER PLAYERS SIGNED PROFESSIONAL CONTRACTS
- 27 FORMER PLAYERS PLAYED IN THE MLB
- FORMER PRESIDENT OF THE ABCA
- AUTHOR OF THE BASEBALL PLAYBOOK

Many refer to you as the "Father of SEC Baseball" as you are, by far, the winningest coach in the history of all sports in the SEC. Talk about what the SEC means to you and the legacy that you left within it.

Polk: Well when I started, I took the job at Mississippi State during the winter of 1975. Baseball was almost an afterthought to the athletic directors and the presidents of the 10 universities. I always thought that baseball had the chance to become very special, because of the natures of the schools in our league, and the weather components since we were all in the Southeast. Other than Kentucky basketball, basketball was somewhat of an afterthought too. I really thought that baseball had the oppurtunity to become something really special.

We really had 12 rules in the NCAA that the Southeastern Conference didn't recognize that were discriminatory about college baseball. SEC had rules that affected the number of games and practices and who we could and could not recruit. I called them the 'dirty dozen' and as a young coach I went after them hard. I went after them in our coaches meetings, and also during my communication with the athletic directors. And, we finally eliminated all of the 12 rules, so we then followed the same rules as the NCAA.

From then on, I was the only full-time college baseball coach in the SEC. The rest of the coaches in our league had other jobs. Most of them were football recruting coordinators, another guy was an equipment manager for all sports. They had all kinds of jobs. So, when I took the job at Mississippi State, I worked full time without any teaching responsibilities and I had a full-time assistant coach. I had no other responsibilites. We started to really take off. When we got a tarp, everybody got a tarp and when we built a new stadium, everybody started building a new stadium.

I was the young guy on the block and because of that, after 31 years of coaching at Georgia and Mississipi State we accumulated a lot of wins, but we also accumulated a lot of losses. What people don't understand is that, although I may have more wins than anybody else in the Southeastern Conference, I also have more losses. I'm not sure how many other coaches in our league will survive 31 years in a very tough and competitive league. We've seen it rise from almost nothing to probably the top baseball conference in the country, in regard to the crowds, the facilities, the winning percentages, College World Series apperances and College World Series wins.

You've been to Omaha 8 times in 5 different decades. What do you think are some of the secrets to your success in college baseball?

Polk: My first one was Georgia Southern, a program that was struggling in Division 2. It became a Division 1 program. Basically, I decided to try to turn it around really quick by recruiting the Florida junior college ranks. I did a pretty good job of bringing in some great players quickly. We went to the College World Series in 1973, my second year. When I was at Georgia, we also went to the College World Series in my second year. With Mississippi State, we went 6 other times and we came in 2nd 7 times so we came very close to going to the College World Series also. As a graduate assistant in 1966, my first coaching job at the University of Arizona as the 3rd-base coach at the age of 22, we went to the College World Series. Technically, I've been there for 5 decades with teams and enjoyed the experience. I also enjoyed the fact that Omaha, like the Southeastern Conference, has grown rapidly since I was first there in 1966 with the Arizona team.

My record is a longevity record, basically the longer that you coach the more wins that you will get and also the more losses that you're going to get, and if you play well the more championships you might have.

You spent 7 summers with the USA National Baseball Team. What are some of your greatest memories from those tours?

Polk: I was involved with 2 Olympics; 1988 in Seoul, we won the gold medal. I was the assistant coach and Mark Marquess from Stanford was the head coach. In 1995-1996, our summer team toured getting prepared for the Atlanta Olympics. We didn't win the gold medal although we played well. Then I was the head coach of the Pan-American team twice. My 7 tours with the USA National team allowed me to meet more coaches and work with the best student athletes in the country.

Then, the Olympics decided that amateurism was no longer viable, so professional athletics took over the Olympics. Baseball was the last bastion of hope to keep the amateurs alive. In Seoul and Atlanta, we played with college kids against veteran teams from all over the world. They decided to scrap the USA team with regard to international play. We toured for 3-4 weeks, although there wasn't much purpose since baseball had been eliminated from the Olympics, which is unfortunate. I really enjoyed getting to explore all the venues around this country and on the international level. I enjoyed working with great baseball players, who were mostly freshmen and sophomores because we were very leery of putting on our roster the draft eligible guys, except for the Olympics when Major League Baseball gave us an exemption where we could use draft eligible guys that could agree to a contract. All of their money had to be put in escrow at the comissioner's office so they would still be amateurs since they hadn't been paid. Subsequently, we got the chance to work with the very best players in college baseball. It was great experience and learning experience for me.

You got to work with some of the best players in the country with those teams, along with so many big leaguers that came from Mississippi State. Is there anything that stands out to you that those guys all had in common?

Polk: Jon Papelbon wasn't highly recruited out of high school and redshirted his first year because he wasn't ready for the SEC. He was a 1B/P and we finally made him a pitcher, and then he progressed rapidly in the Southeastern Conference. He signed a contract as a 4th-rounder and now he's doing very well as one of the premier closers in professional baseball. The other ones were very good. We were very fortunate to get them to come because many of them were drafted out of high school but decided to test the waters in college. Because of that, they had great careers and went on to do very well in pro baseball.

During my time at Mississippi State, we had 8 first round draft picks and most of those guys were not drafted very high or not even at all in high school. I think the fact that they went to college and got at least 3 years of experience under their belt academically and signed contracts in almost all cases before their eligibility was used up.

The Baseball Playbook is the leading textbook on teaching the game of baseball to coaches and players around the world. What inspired you to write this book?

Polk: I always had a playbook. I had one at Georgia Southern, a very minimal publication that I never sold. I wanted the kids to have their hands on, before practice, what we had in mind that day, including all of our bunt defenses, 1st-and-3rd plays, pickoff plays, and offensive plays. I typed it up myself and presented it to the players, so that they could study it. It was actually like another coach for me because I could tell them their homework assignment for tomorrow is all of our pick plays at second base to be prepared so I didn't have to spend valuable practice time explaining to each player what the system was or what the sign was, what the take-off sign was and how we were going to execute it. So, then we could spend most of our time doing that and make corrections as it happened.

In my early years as a head coach, I used to do so many clinics and so I always told high school, college and youth coaches that the kids needed something like a geography, English, or math book and a homework assignment to be prepared for tomorrow. I had never heard of anybody in baseball that has a textbook for their players. The book had signals and everything so anybody that was slow to grasp information could pratice it the night before and keep reading it. We seldom missed signals or assignments because basically, they had a textbook in hand.

While I was travelling around speaking, I was telling everybody that this is what I do, this is the book that my players use. I had many coaches telling me that they would like a copy. I had to tell them that it was just something that I did for my teams and that there wasn't actually a book that I could give them. I also had a man tell me that he would pay anything for the book. So then I took the typewritten book that I had for my team and spent about two years in development. I wrote two pages a day. I'm not a writer, I didn't really enjoy doing it, but it became a 520 page book. It covers everything from the first meeting, to how to train a first-base or a third-base coach, to how to put a sprinkler system in to every aspect of offense/defense and player evaluation.

Once it was complete, I sent a free complimentary book to everyone who was in college baseball and teaching a baseball coaching theory class. I also made a test manual, so that they didn't have to worry about the questions. And, all of a sudden we cornered the market and I was a publisher. Publishing companies wanted the book, but I just did the job for them. We kept selling and selling, and eventually sold 105,000 books. We sold them without any advertising, and without using the internet.

A gentleman in Birmingham now helps me to sell the books online.

Before this, I did all it by hand. I built, packaged, boxed and stamped the books. I did everything from my house and subsequently, I became a publishing company while being a head baseball coach which made it very, very difficult. But, it was important to me that if people were looking for a book that covered all of the aspects of baseball, that this is the one that they needed to have. Nowadays, very few baseball coaching classes are offered in colleges anymore, so our book sales have dropped dramatically because 90% of my sales were in college bookstores and since they didn't have that class anymore the book was dropped.

Where can the readers pick up a copy of the Baseball Playbook?

Polk: If you Google 'Baseball Playbook', it should come up.

SKIP BERTMAN

LEGENDARY COLLEGE BASEBALL COACH AND FORMER ATHLETIC DIRECTOR AT LSU

- REACHED THE COLLEGE WORLD SERIES 11 TIMES

- WON 5 NATIONAL CHAMPIONSHIPS FROM 1991-2000

- HEAD COACH OF THE 1996 US OLYMPIC TEAM

- NAMED NATIONAL COACH OF THE YEAR 6 TIMES

- SERVED AS ATHLETIC DIRECTOR AT LSU FROM 2001-2010

- INDUCTED INTO COLLEGE BASEBALL HALL OF FAME IN 2006

Talk a little bit about what led you to the decision to become the athletic director at LSU following your coaching career.

Bertman: They needed me at LSU in terms of the fact they really didn't have another guy and the chancellor saying, "How about doing us a favor? You know what to do." And I said okay.

You won 5 national championships in one decade, what are some of the keys to winning in Omaha?

Bertman: I think there is a lot of good fortune that you have got to have when you get to Omaha. The best team of players always wins, not the best players but the best team and everybody has to be together. Everybody has to have a certified goal and I think probably that is the best way to go. Nothing substitutes for better athletes. I think we all know that is the number one thing in coaching. But in Omaha, you really do have to zero in on a couple of things. One would be really focus.

What is it like to have the field at LSU named after you after such a successful career coaching there?

Bertman: It was nice that they could do that at LSU. That is always a good feeling, but you don't go into coaching to see how many you can win, how many kids you can help or how many items you can come up with that can help the few play for you. So, naming the field was nice. Very nice!

Tell us about Teamwork, LLC and what you are doing with your motivational speaking now that you have retired as the athletic director.

Bertman: I have always done motivational speaking. I probably do about 25 a year and now mostly through Teamwork, which is a limited liability corporation that I started, that sometimes helps people get where they are going, sometimes offers information depending upon what they need so I will consult for two or three, probably four different clients, as well.

ADDITIONAL VIP RESOURCES

Available at
MentalGameVIP.com

.

COACHING
Q&A

What inspired you to become a coach? Why did you coach?

Bertman: Well a lot of times, a lot of the great coaches, their fathers were coaches. Bill Belicheck, Nick Saban and so many other great ones, their fathers were coaches and of course that really helped them. That wasn't my case. My case was I enjoyed my high school coach and what he did and I thought that I wanted to coach. I worked with kids when they were young in the recreation department so I had the opportunity to do that. Then I had a great desire to be a coach, found out what it would take and what would be needed and, of course, I went ahead and did that.

Polk: I played in high school and then at Grand Canyon University. Then I went to the University of Arizona on a graduate assistantship to teach physical education classes while I was working on my masters degree. One day, I got the guts to go into Frank Sancet's office and ask him if he needed some help out there and he said 'Yeah, we could certainly use you.' At 22 years of age, I was a third-base coach. I did a lot of things I never dreamed I'd do at that age. That got me excited about the possibility that maybe I could do this for a living.

From there I went to the University of New Mexico to get my doctorate degree after being in the Marine Corps Reserve in Vietnam War. After that, I went to Miami Dade Junior College-South. I had a good friend ask me to come down there to be an assistant coach, and then Georgia Southern asked me to be the head coach. After that, I went to Mississippi State, Georgia and then back to Mississippi State. Now, I'm enjoying my experience working for my former assistant coach Brian Shoop, who was with me there at State for 7 years. I actually asked him if he wanted me to come over and be a volunteer coach at UAB.

In order for me to keep my good feeling about working with the best baseball players in the country, I've decided to use my summers to go up to the Cape Cod League. Since I'm a volunteer coach, I'm not allowed to recruit, so there's not much for me to do in the summer time so I took that responsibility on as well, so I'm staying pretty busy for an old guy.

Did you have core values, standards, or expectations for your teams while you were a head coach?

Polk: I never set goals for the players, but they knew what their responsibilities were, both on the field and off. They were written in the book. The book had the requirements in regard to class attendance and tardiness. I always surrounded myself with outstanding coaches. One of the things we are more proud of than anything else is that 5 of my assistant coaches at various schools have become President of the American Baseball Coaches Association, and I'm more proud of this than anything else. I wanted to surround myself with not just good assistant coaches, but also good managers and trainers. I wanted to have role-models that the players could emulate. I told them we're going to do the very best we can every day, on and off the field. You don't have to set goals, just make every day an important experience, both for themselves and their families.

Bertman: Our values, I would say, are pretty much like everybody else in coaching probably any sport. In particular baseball, there was nothing fancy. Everybody got there on time, everybody tried as hard as they could, all the values and rules pretty much that would make parents happy today were followed, not because that would make the parents happy so much as that is the right thing to do.

How did you motivate your team and get them all moving in the same direction?

Bertman: I probably used "motivation" more than others. I would use a video, either a 5-8 minute video, before every game and the video would have something to do with baseball or something like baseball or something that had a message that I wanted the boys to receive. I think that teaching from screen is important today, with kids using screens as they do. I told a different story before every game. I had some other motivational techniques that were used and they worked for me. You can only do what works for you.

I am going to give you one example of a story, if you take them to right or left field whichever dugout you are closer to, as a learning experience. A good teaching time is before the game. Everyone is worried about, "Will I make the error? Will I hit the winning run?" I think that is a good time. Everybody wants to play, and you are 7-8 minutes away from the game. If we played Friday and Saturday and we won, I came up with a story, in this case Rocky Marciano, a boxer who was 49-0 and could really take a punch and obviously deliver one. And he is from Rockton, Mass and somebody who wanted to be a baseball player but really wasn't good enough so he became a boxer.

I would go on. The story takes 2-3 minutes. I would wait for a lot of eye contact. What that story would deliver would be, "Don't be satisfied with two wins." Let's knock them out the third day. That was an example of what the stories would be so they would be stories that had a meaning to that day.

Polk: I've never had any signs in the locker room, slogans or posters in the dugout. I felt as though I couldn't get motivated by that so I didn't think the players could either. I think the motivation I inspired to them is that if you have the aspiration to get a degree, if you want to play professional baseball then I've got a plan. I've got coaches with me that can help you achieve that goal.

Thankfully, at Mississippi State, we had early success that turned into more success, which meant that we had bigger and better crowds. We were the first ones to have an extensive radio network and the first to have my own TV show once a week. We told the players that we would put them in the best uniform we could, that they would play in the best venues we can, and that we wanted them to look like first class, All-American young men in the way that they handled themselves and looked. I told them I was going to provide them with these opportunities, and that it was their opportunity to be successful and that if they didn't take advantage of it, then it was their problem and not mine.

What does the 'it' factor look like? When a kid has it, how do you harness and empower it?

Polk: I did so much recruting in my early years and I don't miss it at all because of the time involved. Now that I'm a volunteer coach, I'm not allowed to. I always valued my judgement when I watch a kid coming on and off of the field, how he handles adversity, how he handled success, and watched him in all components of the game. I think that the 'It' factor is athleticim, strength, bat-speed, body language, and overall command and speed for pitchers.

You have to ask yourself if they look like a boy you want to have in your program for 4 or 5 years, and if they have the ability to develop the skills that they had in high school or junior college, and you just have to 'pull the trigger'. One of the reasons we were so successful was because we were able to out-recruit other schools that had more money and a higher tradition. At the same time, we felt like we made some great decisions on players, and because of that, we won some games.

Bertman: Well let's say the 'It' factor in baseball is the guy who comes through all the time, the guy that can make the big play, in any sport, but in this case baseball. I would say the 'It' factor, number one, he has a lot of talent. There has to be the guy that runs fast, throws well, pitches well or he hits well. There is usually a lot of talent.

I would say secondly, there is usually personality. They are usually well liked, personally.

Three, I would say they are pretty smart. They are usually reasonable students, but even beyond that they have a lot of street smarts.

Lastly, but most importantly, I would say the 'It' guy has a team attitude more than a 'me' attitude, and that is what makes him so accessible to everyone around him.

What was your recruiting philosophy?

Bertman: I am really guilty in that I wasn't a really good recruiter. I did have some good assistants that were pretty good recruiters. I wasn't much of a 'go after them' guy because they are stars, or somebody you had to call. I wanted mostly kids that wanted to come, and mostly we did, we had kids who would come from locally and you can build them over a period of time.

One of the questions not on your list that I think is really important is 'Let's redshirt that freshman.' One that isn't going to be a great player and he is not going to be in the major leagues. He has probably got over four years before he graduates from college, so I think redshirting is a good thing. I think then, ultimately, when he is 21-22, he is able to do pretty much anything and baseball not being that particular difficult at the college level unlike big league level. So, he could play.

So mostly the recruiting was: let's take a guy, anybody who could play, keep them for one year, sometimes two years, before they would actually play and then later on they could become good players.

I did a lot of that and I would say it was more common before because you could have any number, say 42-47 kids as opposed to 35 that they use now which is a horrible rule. It's a terrible rule to have to tell somebody you can't play. It is just kind of a stupid NCAA thing.

Polk: One of the biggest things is that when we brought players in for a visit, we always talked to the student hosts after they had left. We wanted to find out what they thought of the player and also how he had communicated with the other players. We spent very little time with the recruits. We basically turned them over to the ballclub and let them interact with that young man. We were very conscious of the fact that we wanted a player who could represent himself and his family in a first class manner. We wanted other families to know that if their son came to our school, then he would be around good quality kids. The moral factors were important and also how the player handled himself, how the player interacted with us and his family and also how his family interacted with him.

During some of the home visits that I took, I was looking for a player who had family support. I also wanted the player to have a good family-oriented philosophy that he could take from his family into our family. We always considered ourselves a family, even though the family was disrupted after 4 years.

'Is this the type of young man that I want to be around?' I want to guarantee the parents if that young boy joins our family, he will leave our program a better man than we received him as compliments from their family.

Who were the mentors or coaches that made the greatest impact on your life? What is one thing that you learned from them?

Polk: Being in international baseball, we always had a different status of coaches. Frank Sancet was the first one. I never dreamed that as I walked into his office I'd become the University of Arizona's third-base coach at the age of 22. Also, Bob Lee at New Mexico gave me responsibilities. Charlie Green, the legendary coach at Miami Dade Junior College, let me do my thing.

Then Skip Bertman and I were together for 3 summer tours. When you talk about summer tours, we're talking about long summers. With the 1988 Olympic Team, we gathered in Millington, Tennessee, on the first of June and we didn't return home until the end of September. The Seoul Olympics were at the end of September. We had to get a waivers from the NCAA that the kids could miss their fall schedule and still be eligible for the spring. Mark Marquess of Stanford was the head coach of the 1988 team.

There's just so many coaches that I have been around, just being around them, watching what they do with the players and how they interact with the players, and the ways in which they teach. It's all molded me into who I am today and that is an old coach that is still hanging around.

Bertman: I had two mentors. One of them, Ron Fraser, the coach of the University of Miami, who was really the great mentor for me because I like to teach fine points, teach everything and make the players into coaches if that is what they would want to do. I'd want to do all of that, so if there is six pick off ways to second base, I'd do all six of them. In reality that is not going to win you one more ball game by having six pick off plays at second base but if I had three guys that could steal home, I could teach them how to steal home. That too is probably not going to win very many ball games.

You know some of the lower percentage things I was allowed to do by Ron Fraser and that was good. He was mostly into promotion of the game and, of course, a foreseer of the game being much better than it was. A long time ago, he was into crowds and he did a great job and showed me pretty much how to promote and raise money. I think that was one guy.

Then I had an earlier guy at a young age name Max Sappeur, who was a former professional player who worked at the Recreational Department who taught me things about baseball when I was 14-15 that were usually taught to people who were, I would say, professionals and gave me an opportunity and I had a different view. So I was lucky, I had a lot of good people.

How did you balance your personal and professional life with the demands of being a head baseball coach?

Polk: When the book first came about, it was a trying time. I was spending a lot of time on it, and I didn't want it to hurt what I was doing at the various schools I was at. I also did a lot of speaking and never charged anybody at the high school, junior college or college a speaking fee. If I had to fly or stay in a hotel, they'd pick that up. And then with the recruiting, if I had a day off, then I would practice and would head out to watch a baseball game. I was a road warrior.

The good thing about being at the University of Alabama at Birmingham is that I have more free time than I had ever had before and as you get older you should probably enjoy that more. I didn't have any major hobbies. I was just a young guy that got captivated by recruiting and coaching. And then I told myself that if I was going to do a good job for myself, my kids and coaches then I should put a full day's effort in. I became what most coaches would commonly refer to as a 'workaholic' and I think that is good, but sometimes it's not good. Basically, I was a full-time college baseball coach. Believe me!

Bertman: Well let's make this perfectly clear, the only coach that really has 14 hours a day at work is a football coach at college. There isn't anybody else. Even the basketball coach doesn't need to worry too much about it, but when you get down to baseball and tennis and golf and swimming and the others, I mean, come on, let's face it. There is regular school, 1 ½ - 2 hours of practice, and there is the rest of the day so I don't say there is much balance.

If you want to ask that question, obviously that could only be asked to a football coach who actually has time, sometimes sixteen hours a day, and naturally they do have to put a lot of balance. Baseball is pretty easy.

How long were the practices that you held at LSU? Were they different or the same duration of time and how would you decide what was needed?

Bertman: What was needed would be most likely. High percentage things like batting practice, hitting the ball, practicing pitching, another high percentage outcome of the game was used every day. Run downs and other things that were low percentage in wins and losses were also practiced, but pretty much whatever was needed.

What does it take to be a great baseball coach?

Polk: Everybody says that kids are changing. I see that a little bit. The high tech stuff still confounds me a lot. They are slightly more self-indulgent, egotistical and pampered by youth coaches, showcases and travel ball. The good thing about coaching in college, rather than in high school, is the fact that you got the opportunity to bring in players from outside of the area. You have to make good decisions about who to bring into the program. Some people would say you should get some juvenile diliquents who can hit the ball a long way. I would say, well if you can't hit the ball a long way, I want a nice kid who can gap the ball or hit balls in the 4 and 6 hole. That is why I enjoy being around Brian Shoop and his staff at the UAB because they recruit kids that I would recruit and they do not just dump kids based on their performance.

I'm not going to get into my battles with the NCAA, but they started to damage college baseball in regard to so many avenues. They didn't have any respect for our game, and yet we are the second largest producer of revenue for the NCAA Championships. I was the lead guy fighting the NCAA, and also organizing the override and veto votes. I was doing it all as a full-time coach. I survived on little sleep, and I just thought that if nobody else was going to do it, then I can guarantee that I will get it done because it was wrong. The NCAA was an evil organization to baseball and it continues to be that way. We have 7 sanctions that no other sport has. Baseball is a clean sport, it's the national pastime and I figured if no one else was going to do it, I was going to give it an effort.

I lost the battle and retired from Mississippi State with 3 years left on my contract because I knew if I stayed there, I'd have to do one thing that I never dreamed I'd ever do which is dump kids based on performance. With a squad limit of 35, we're the only sport that has a roster restrcition. That is why I wear #35 at UAB as a protest number. 99.9% of people who see me with #35 on have no idea why, but I'm just one of those guys that when something is wrong and someone is hurting our sport, then I have to stand up for and fight them.

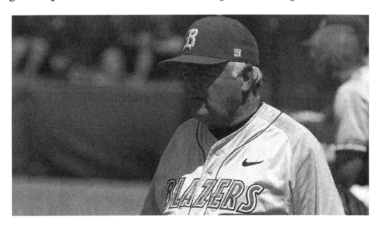

Bertman: Over the years, a number close to fifty, I get asked this by kids. "Oh I'd like to do that. I'd like to be a coach." But you've got to be lucky to be at the right school at the right time. I think I'm proud of baseball growing, you know I would say that is the proudest thing, the fact a baseball coach makes a lot of money today or gets a lot of attention is a good thing compared to thirty years ago. I think that people who want to do this find that there is no test to see if you are going to be any good or not at this, kind of like parenting; there is no test. I find an awful lot of kids fail even though they know a lot of baseball fundamentals, they are not as good teachers as they should be. They ought to be good teachers. They have got to have a plan, like a six week plan for a teacher. Those kinds of plans for a baseball coach make the difference. They have got to have some sensibility and some resourcefulness. When they see something, they have high antenna. They see that it means something and then they put it into their book.

So I've seen kids and watched them train for years and years and years, they are just very average coaches and yet they know quite a bit but they are missing really the 'It' factor for coaching. They just don't seem to have that 'zip' factor. You can see so many of those guys in other sports too. It is a hard thing to get; it is a hard thing to explain.

What is your proudest moment? Why?

Bertman: The proudest moments are watching the game grow. I think that is the proudest moment, watching the people need tickets to get in to see a college game. I think a full house makes money, not for the coach, but for the school. I think that is a proud moment for me.

Polk: I've been in the World Series 8 times and didn't win it. My good friend Mike Martin at Florida State has been there longer than that and never won it. I think my proudest moment is achieving the success to take the kids and their families to 'the ultimate', which is the College World Series in Omaha, Nebraska. I've lost final games to go to Omaha. I'm the type of guy that if I have to get in an argument with an umpire, if we lose then we should just get up the next day, work harder and see if we can do it again.

The whole key to coaching is you've got to make a commitment. It's not easy. It's a tough life, but at the same time it's enjoyable. Some coaches put too much pressure on themselves to win. I never put pressure on kids to win, I just said 'Hey, go out and compete. If we lose, the better team won that day. We might have been the best team, but we weren't the best team that particular day.' I put losses behind me very quick. People say that when you shake hands with me at the end of the game, then you can't tell if I've won or lost. That's my nature and at the age of 71, I'm not going to change now.

MILLION DOLLAR QUESTION

What do you know now that you wish you knew before your coaching career?

Bertman: I don't know. I don't think I'm in that category. I think I knew a lot when I started. I thought I probably knew more than I did. I was very confident, but later I found out I'm not as smart as they could pitch or they could play and I was a better coach when I had better players.

When I started, I started different than a lot of guys. I was little league coach, moved up the pony league, American league, junior high school, junior college, college. I was different than most people. I didn't just jump in, so I had a little bit of time from the mentors.

Polk: When I was a young guy, after being at University of Arizona and New Mexico, I decided that what I will be is a coach; not knowing at what level. I just never dreamed that being successful in college baseball woul require the amount of work it did, both on and off the field. I think that almost 90% of my day, throughout the whole year, was not at practice or games. It was mainly alumni relationships, phone calls, answering letters, doing public relations, and handling staff. It's just constant.

What I've learned that I didn't realize when I started was that if you're going to do it well, you have to have a great work ethic. If you're not going to put the time in, it's not going to get done.

HOT SEAT

Bringin' The Heat!

OMAHA

Polk: The Ultimate.

Bertman: The place to be.

MENTAL GAME

Bertman: Very important but physical is important too.

Polk: I'm not into the mental game very much, so I can't come up with a word!

STRENGTH & CONDITIONING

Polk: Overuse.

Bertman: The stronger you are, the better chance you have of hitting the ball better.

MLB DRAFT

Bertman: Draft is good, Major League Baseball is good.

Polk: Adjustments need to be made.

HITTING

Polk: Two words: bat speed.

Bertman: Hard to teach. If I had something to tell: recruit somebody that has always been a good hitter since he has been in Little League. Very tough to teach hitting. Instead, make them better offensive players.

PITCHING

Bertman: Easier to teach. Working with people over a period of time, I'd be shocked, stunned and amazed that anybody can't pitch after a period of time with a good coach.

Polk: Strikes.

DEFENSE

Polk: Routine.

Bertman: Ah, I like it. I like dominant pitching first, hitting second and defense third to win a champonship.

BBCOR

Polk: Putrid.

Bertman: BBCOR was a reaction, a typical NCAA stupid move that made baseball worse for 2 years. Now it's a lot better since they changed the ball. Naturally, they won't change the bat any in fear of lawsuits, which drives them up a wall. BBCOR is no good.

THE
CONCLUSION

Recommended Reading for Baseball Players & Coaches

Polk: The Baseball Playbook, for sure. I've read many baseball books and they are good, but coaches have to make their own decisions. When I first started coaching I had maybe 25 pick plays at second base and then in a game, I didn't know if they remember what we have. So, I tried to keep it as simple as possible, because it can be complicated. I'm always trying to devise ways to make things easier for player, so that when they step on the field, and when things happen in the game, they can say they've been there before. That's when I devised the fundamental drill series 1 and 2, so that we could do drills every day in 3 or 4 minute segments so that we could cover all aspects of the defensive part of the game and that's been a very important part of my coaching experience. The game is fast. It's a game where there is some downtime but there's concentration involved. We basically practice things that happen over and over again so when they happen in a game, the kids can say 'I've been there before.' That doesn't mean they won't make an error or a bonehead play, but at the same time they feel comfortable. We basically practice things that happen over and over again. Trick plays are nice to work on, offense and defense, but let's work on things that happen often, such as fly ball communication, infield defense, communication in the 4 hole and 6 hole, put a couple pick plays in, maybe a couple crazy plays that you can do occasionally like we have done at UAB, just to let the other team know that they are in a battle here because our kids are prepared to win.

Bertman: Sports Gene by David Epstein is a really good book for a coach of any sport particularly, but baseball for sure.

Advice for Young, Aspiring Baseball Coaches

Polk: Be yourself. Don't look at Skip Bertman, Ron Polk, Mike Martin, Augie Garrido or anybody else and say that's what I want to be. Be what you are. You're going to have to understand that this is not an easy profession. If you're going to be successful (not so much wins and losses), when people say that guy can coach and that guy is a role model for my kids. It takes a lot of work, it's a lot of dedication and if you're in it just for the money, or because you want to win some championships or rings. Then, get out of the profession and give it to someone else. Allow some else who cares about kids, and playing the game right to come in there and represent themselves on and off of the field in the best way that they possibly can.

ADDITIONAL VIP RESOURCES

Available at

MentalGameVIP.com

ADDITIONAL VIP RESOURCES

Available at

LeadershipVIP.com

FOR MORE FROM MATT MORSE,
VISIT MATT-MORSE.COM!